HOLY
WORK

MARSHA SINETAR

HOLY WORK

Be love. Be blessed.
Be a blessing.

A Crossroad Book
The Crossroad Publishing Company
New York

The Crossroad Publishing Company
370 Lexington Avenue, New York, NY 10017

Printed in the United States of America

Library of Congress Cataloging-in-Publication Data
Sinetar, Marsha.
    Holy work : be love, be blessed, be a blessing / Marsha Sinetar.
      p. cm.
    Includes bibliographical references.
    ISBN 0-8245-1759-8
    1. Work – Religious aspects – Christianity – Meditations.
    2. Devotional calendars.   I. Title.
    BV4593.S56 1998
    242'.68 – dc21   98-18481

1   2   3   4   5   6   7   8   9   10   02   01   00   99   98

And the Spirit and the bride say, Come.
And let him that heareth say, Come.
And let him that is athirst come.
And whosoever will, let him take the water of life freely.

(REVELATION 22:17)

Introductory Words

Only God is holy. Only work that reflects God's divine nature is holy. Our vocation — that summons to grow distinctively whole by means of our innate nature and talents — lets us honor and glorify God's gifts to us. A vocation reflects God's will *in* us, and our love for God. It draws us to God in intimate oneness and — through our efforts — it's as if, in a very real sense, we sing our praises unto the Lord. This book proposes that there is an inherent holiness in any true calling: boat building, computer repair, banking, or traveling around the world in "retirement." Readers who unabashedly love God already sense this. Intuitively they know that love expressed productively somehow transfigures them, works Love's perfect will in them, and transfigures life into a consecrated journey toward the Divine.

That sacred movement involves "vocation" — work that lets us commune with whatever is highest and best, makes us want to honor God, or help others, setting aside our own plans and egoism and yielding all to the Spirit of Truth's industry *in* us. Readers who love God also sense that such surrender is more fulfillment than self-denial. A vocation wholly occupies us with the natural and supernatural sweetness of everyday life. Progressively, life unfolds our true self. This brings to mind the words of St. Francis de Sales, "Be the self you are, and be that perfectly."

We often suppose that to be valid, a vocation is expressed only in people with a formal religious call. This is not precisely accurate. Three benchmarks of all vocations, writes Fr. Roch Kereszty, are (a) love for God, (b) love for people, and (c) the willingness to grow from mistakes.[1] A vocation flows from the depths of our stillness, our essential purity of heart or core being. Each human possesses such a core, an essential transcendent silence. Not all acknowledge vocation in language, functional terms, or a way of being that honors the intimacy between what they do and who they are as God's first fruit.[2] With a vocation our gifts and inclinations matter. We will, and somehow do, turn these over to a deep primordial summons. Our vocation instills in us a longing to *be* what we are, to reflect the light that's in us, to give over our gifts, capabilities, even our limits and peculiarities to the movement of the interior Spirit.

This is, to be sure, frequently inconvenient. It is also a universal response of a divine yearning to be fruitful, to experience a reflexive oblation for — and communion with — Life itself. Ahead of usefulness, before service to others or "success," comes trustful intimacy, connectedness, and oneness, with the Spirit of love. We do not exploit a vocation for our own glory, nor use work to construct an edifice of fame or fortune; rather we yield up who we are and what we do to become a cell in Life's living body — to glorify the house of God's glory (Isa. 60:7). Not just an elite few are called in this fashion. Many are summoned. Many more could be "partakers of a heavenly calling" to be used of the Lord, if they would but listen *inwardly* and with discernment.

Ways to Use This Book

This slim volume of meditations links the way we work and the work we *are* as God's workmanship. It suggests that our daily labor, approached rightly, devotionally, can help us come into our fullness of being as unique individuals within the unit of a larger existence. Ultimately — as we affirm God's summons — we become willing servants of Life's purposes, and not only our daily work but we ourselves reflect that which is of God's infinitude. As a friend told me, "A spiritual teacher of mine once cautioned me, 'Your work will not bring you joy. *You* must bring your joy to your work.'"

The meditations in this book are organized into three sections: *What? How? Why?* Each short passage is designed for use as a *week-long* musing. Each highlights a central theme, a verse of Scripture, and a few open-ended journal inquiries in the hope that readers might start or end their day by chewing on these.

The purpose of the journal exercises is to help us *actualize* the meditations — to make them a part of our lives.

Of course, these reflective exercises are optional. You may find that rereading the meditation throughout the week is sufficient to ignite a growthful movement of awareness. Or you may prefer a pen-and-paper method to capture elusive insights. Consider the value of repeating not only each meditation, but each journal exercise, perhaps on a clean piece of paper every time, each exercise for seven days — say, from Sunday to Sunday — at approximately the same time of day to habituate yourself to a reflective inquiry into *Holy Work* as it relates to your own life. Should the habit support your wholesome growth, you might transfer it to other spiritual readings or purposes.

The three sections explore...

I. What: What is holy work?

Part I investigates the term "vocation." The meditations suggest that when any endeavor (formally religious or not; paid or not) ties us to God and others in love, service, and effective functioning, it is a devotional, wholly spiritual operation, prayer — executed in the secret recesses of our heart. Frequently thought of as an inner call, a vocation summons each one distinctively.

II. How: How might we find our vocation?

Part II addresses selected "how to" concerns. In a nutshell, a vocation flows from wholeness — not that we are "finished" or fully complete, but that *tending* toward wholeness we hear inwardly. We feel a prompting to be real — to be what we were created to be. Aligning our thoughts, choices, and life with God's thoughts, with Scripture's sensibilities (which, after all, are not like our usual thoughts) quickens that tendency, that substantive coming to life, as simply ourselves. Hence the logic of the meditations in this book: It is healing to our flesh, as well as to the enfleshing of our affairs, to chew up and assimilate the Word of God.

Reflecting on Scripture regularly lets us hear our inner

summons, the Spirit within. Eventually confidence grows —
along with faith. With willing self-abandon, we cheerfully
discipline our gifts in our progressive service to self and
other. Apprehending our vocation requires innocent open-
ness to pressing interior cues. Scripture calls the sum total
of these cues "wisdom," and wisdom invites us to be fully
engaged, occupied, and committed in faith to a worshipful
path. Worship, intimate communion with God, leads the way
to vocation — and this is far beyond obligatory "service" in a
prosaic sense. All vocations ask us to walk by faith, not sight.

III. Why: Why bother?

Part III discusses the blessings of a vocation. Benefits flow
to us when we dedicate ourselves to a vocation. Any artist
or inventor who works with singleminded intent understands
this. A sense of oblation, devotedness, commitment, intimate
trusting oneness with God — these bring *us* to life. Yet we
who receive both spiritual and material compensation from
our endeavors know that, in being blessed, we also become a
blessing to others. That is true giving, not of our doing exactly, and a reciprocity of good that is a vivid feature of any
vocation: Whatever truly sparks our unique genius — and
everyone has that spark, if only in dormant condition — rewards us, and that reward somehow orchestrates the collective
good on a wider, universal scale.

Our conscious, freely chosen commitment to love God
in everyday life expresses supernatural attributes — intuition or discernment, cheerfulness, courage, compassion —

transfiguring *us* into a holy work. At first, our simple daily service can reflect whatever is fitted to our nature. Later, we change. Discords lessen, fulfillments expand, and we may well find ourselves undertaking tasks that previously seemed beyond us, far above our natural talents. As Oswald Chambers reminds us, "God's call is expressive of His nature; consequently when I receive His nature and hear His call, the voice of the Divine nature sounds in both and the two work together."[3] That call speaks of oneness, the sacred oneness for which we thirst.

About Words and Work

Aside from the Bible verses, mostly quoted from the King James Version, I've employed universal synonyms for the word "God," thereby skirting gender-specific references in the meditations themselves. The word "God," as Raimon Panikkar has pointed out, is an invocation. Precisely in that fashion, a vocation is, to me, prayer — praise for whatever's holy. Indeed, who has not felt that adoration from time to time, while carving a chunk of wood or clipping a child's toenails, sighing along with the psalmist:

> *Bless the Lord, O my soul,*
> *and all that is within me, bless his holy name . . .*
>
> (PSALM 103:1–2)

O, Lord, how manifold are thy works!
in wisdom hast thou made them all:
the earth is full of thy riches . . .
the Lord shall rejoice in his works.

(PSALM 104:24–31)

Another key to vocation is that it invites our *direct* experience of true wealth: Wholeness. Sufficiency. Those of us who feel summoned by a vocation *feel* enriched. We dwell in subjective harmony. We are engaged — occupied — at the deepest level of being. Simultaneously, we glean insights about life's supposed secrets or somehow surmount seeming obstructions — all that even during the hardship, the rejection, the so-called setback. Deeper still than surface happenings is joy, the fruit of the Spirit. Deepest still is love for God.

Ordinary, secular work can actively remunerate us. It can infuse us with feelings of wonder — just for being alive. Work that expresses God's love accomplishes more: It lets us go forth each day, to our diverse jobs, gradually encountering our most minute and private meanings and our largest perfections in God's holiness. Another blessing: That our completion as individuals might be included in God's incomprehensible plan of creation is cause for lasting jubilation (Ps. 104:22–24).

Whatever our life's appearance, whether we labor in a cell or in a global marketplace, any engagement that calls us to the radical heart of Love moves us from death to Life. So come, let us take the water of life freely. Then the voice of a stranger we will not — cannot — follow.

Part I

WHAT CONSTITUTES VOCATION?

The most unspectacular tasks can yield spectacular spiritual fruit — can make us yearn to give up even ourselves — as we employ our gifts and faith to vivify the reality of the Spirit within. A vocation summons each one distinctively. Through our work we can become whole individuals who walk by the light of faith, who live in truth, becoming supernaturally perfected — the light of God.

Paraphrasing William Blake, with a vocation comes our insight that whatever lives is holy and that life delights itself in life. That consciousness of cheer lets us offer up our efforts to the Lord simply as praise, simply as gratitude, simply as joy in being alive and doing what we're born to do.

Unobtrusively, through a vocation the mundane chores and the prestigious activity are reconfigured in love as service and utter gratitude for Life.

> *God is love;*
> *Whoever lives in love, lives in God*
> *and God in him.* (1 JOHN 4:16)

Love's inconvenient prod to love

Beloved, let us love one another . . .

Has virtue, talent, or your own longing to serve others prodded you inconveniently? A vocation calls us out of warm, cozy nests to face our cold unknowns. That is its cue. Vocation asks us to step out willingly and persist with our life's goals. Despite boredom or hardship, we function. We contribute consciously. For Life's sake, we humble ourselves — going to the end of the line, facing criticism, going last if need be, to take our place vibrantly in the scheme of life.

If somehow we find an unexpected harmony in the midst of weariness that, too, reveals vocation. As one man noted: "When in my twenties, I wondered what I'd be and do in later life. Now, at fifty, in good times and supposed setbacks, I realize that what I wanted to do is what I *am* doing."

This is the drill: We let go into Love. We know that we are God's offspring, here and now, created for love — for intimate friendship with Love. We love our daily efforts, not because they are so grand but because, incomprehensibly, they testify that we *are* love. Because before the world existed, we were loved.

Ye are of God, little children, and have overcome them:
because greater is he that is in you, than he that is in the world.
They are of the world: therefore speak they of the world,
and the world heareth them.
We are of God: he that knoweth God heareth us;
he that is not of God heareth not us.
Hereby know we the spirit of truth, and the spirit of error.
Beloved, let us love one another: for love is of God;
and everyone that loveth is born of God.... (1 JOHN 4:4–7)

❦❦❦❦❦❦

Observing the nuances and practical patterns of your every-day life, you may wish to reflect on the following questions (or ones you prefer and create for yourself) during the course of the week . . .

❧ To what extent are you driven or called forth *today?*

❧ What, in your experience, seems to be the difference between being "driven" and being "called" in a physical, emotional, or spiritual sense?

❧ What might it mean for you (or cost you) to consciously choose to honor Life through some line of *natural* endeavor? (That is, what seem to be your natural talents, your working inclinations, and how might you elevate these through your most commonplace or genuine, intuitive choices?)

Becoming a vital cell in the collective body

*Not many mighty,
not many noble, are called...*

Heeding the call of vocation, we become a vital cell in the body of humankind. With high-mindedness and perhaps a touch of divine madness, we grasp the sacred promise in each day's activity. The more we give, the greater our wealth. Each of us has something unique to give. The mother's healing hand on her child's hot brow is soothing, not like the sculptor's rough, calloused grip on cold, hard marble. Yet both hands are enriched and both enrich us.

At best our labors honor and illustrate immutable Life. Whatever seems to disrupt the day we can turn over to God, render it spiritual, in which case all things work together for good. For pilots and plumbers, for gardeners and greengrocers alike, a vocation stirs a dedicated movement toward whatever is lastingly good. It's our way of growing whole — holy — as particular persons, in the context of community. Thus are we all completed in God, yet not "perfected" in the world's eyes. Quite the opposite, sometimes. The question lingers: In what thoughts, words or choices does *your* vitality lay?

Choose your vital expression this day.

For ye see your calling, brethren,
how that not many wise men after the flesh,
not many mighty, not many noble, are called:
But God hath chosen the foolish things of the world to confound
   the wise;
and God hath chosen the weak things of the world to confound
   the things which are mighty;
And base things of the world, and things which are despised,
   hath God chosen,
yea, and things which are not, to bring to nought things that
   are.... (1 CORINTHIANS 1:26–28)

꿍꿍꿍꿍꿍꿍

Observing the nuances and practical patterns of your every-day life, you may wish to reflect on the following questions (or ones you prefer and create for yourself) during the course of the week...

◈ What might it mean to use today's labors, activities, conversations as if these all had "sacred potential"?

◈ What small, daily disruption have you turned over to God today, and what was the result?

◈ What one upcoming, anticipated stress or conflict might you "turn over to God" this week? How, mentally, can you best rehearse that sort of response?

Subjective affluence

*God is able to make all grace
abound toward you . . .*

Does your work bear fruit? Do you trust God or your business contacts for your increase? A vocation reflects a living love, not concern with status, salaries, or pleasing others — although money somehow follows. And in various amounts. Consider three poets. One supports his passion by teaching school. Another prospers in her poetic art by writing verse at night and ads by day. The third works at McDonald's, cooking up rhymes along with burgers.

"Making money" per se is incidental to their vocation. In this, faithfulness and wholesome depths attract what's needed. (They comprehend what Emerson reputedly once said, that money often costs *too* much.) Rewards, fulfillment, perhaps accolades follow the steady, responsible investment of talent, values, and self-discipline. So it is with us.

Who are the worthy way-showers in our field? Those who have gone before have set a vocational pattern for us, if we know how and where to look. Jesus Christ revealed *the* pattern of vocational fitness, taught us to be "fishers of men." Fascination, vivid engrossments, and simple self-forgetting deliver abundant returns. Vocation is Love's enterprise *in* us, and as such it never fails.

Every man according as he purposeth in his heart,
so let him give; not grudgingly, or of necessity:
for God loveth a cheerful giver.
And God is able to make all grace abound toward you;
that ye, always having all sufficiency in all things,
may abound to every good work. . . .

(2 CORINTHIANS 9:7–8)

෯෯෯෯෯෯෯

Observing the nuances and practical patterns of your every-day life, you may wish to reflect on the following questions (or ones you prefer and create for yourself) during the course of the week . . .

- To date, what has been the "fruit" of your work? At the deepest subjective level, for what "fruit" do you yearn?

- How, specifically, might you increase your giving-of-self all this week? (Name at least three ways.)

- What five words or phrases describe your "vivid en-gagements": As you observe yourself and review your fulfillments each day this week, when are you most fully and gladly occupied? Consider keeping a log and reviewing it at week's end.

An inner call to functional wholeness

The joy of the Lord is your strength...

Are we driven or are we summoned forth? Do life's endeavors reveal our soul's spiritual loyalties or dutiful folly? In humorist James Thurber's words, are we "fortune's slave [with] one foot in the gravy, [and] one foot in the grave"?[4] Or are we called out by a hidden love to be who we are, in truth?

To become faithful to our talents and unique disposition means to affirm our inner press for wholeness. That press involves a call, a longing, a quiet, patient invitation to be purely ourselves. Beware the brutal, impolite driver.

This is vocation: That we answer God's call to be and to give of ourselves, in service. That we honor Life intentionally through some line of natural, concrete endeavor: be it bricklaying or basket weaving. The form of work makes no difference. Later, we may be equipped for more. Faithfulness in little things invites larger fare. Display of a vocation is the divine image, burning bright within, and cause for great rejoicing. To affirm that brightness functionally is to grow ever more alive, progressively distinctive and universally disposed. In a nutshell and put simply, each successful vocation celebrates ultimate Reality.

Then he said unto them,
Go your way, eat the fat, and drink the sweet,
and send portions unto them for whom nothing is prepared:
for this day is holy unto our Lord:
neither be ye sorry; for the joy of the Lord is your strength.

(NEHEMIAH 8:10)

❧❧❧❧❧❧

Observing the nuances and practical patterns of your everyday life, you may wish to reflect on the following questions (or ones you prefer and create for yourself) during the course of the week...

❧ As you reflect on this week's meditative passage, what *current* prods to growth inconvenience you? What's your current pattern of response?

❧ What one *persistent* inner press seems to be nudging you out of your comfort zone? How are — or aren't — you listening?

❧ When today , despite weariness, have you felt fulfilled? Name three times when you have loved making an extra effort. What does your daily experience teach you?

Increased spiritual intelligence

Make straight paths for your feet . . .

Not all of us are in love with what we do. Nor are all of us emotionally *ready* for a vocation: the loving, active expression of an anointed Life. Whenever we are financially or emotionally ready, we can create work. (Think of refugees who run fruit stands to survive.)

A vocation, by contrast, is something else again. It asks for, and builds up, different strengths: spiritual intelligence, intuitive clarity, a rich, full heart, courage.

Holy bakers offer up their bread to the poor, holy healers offer hope and health, and holy artists give beauty. All who are vocationally ready send out a spark of light, move beyond the world, and grow brighter, lighter, for it. With time, tenacious practice, and desire, each of us can make love our governing aim. Whether we express our love in solitary or social ways, Love's triumph in each of us marks each work as holy.

Wherefore lift up the hands which hang down, and the feeble knees;

And make straight paths for your feet, lest that which is lame be turned out of the way; but let it rather be healed.

Follow peace with all men, and holiness, without which no man shall see the Lord. (HEBREWS 12:12–14)

෯෯෯෯෯෯

Observing the nuances and practical patterns of your everyday life, you may wish to reflect on the following questions (or ones you prefer and create for yourself) during the course of the week...

෯ As you experience yourself each day this week, what strengths do you seem to require in order to become "emotionally ready" for a vocation? As a unique individual, what does that phrase mean to you?

෯ With what trusted friend, mentor, or guide might you share your vocational ideas, plans, or discouragements? How willing are you to do that? *Name* a trusted mentor of friend.

෯ What frailties, excuses, excesses, or self-sabotaging habits might you need to give up in order that Love might triumph in you, through you? To what degree do you believe you can do that? What does that tell you?

Distinctive service to self and other

*Thou shalt love the Lord, thy God
with all thy heart, soul and mind . . .*

Whatever its outward form, a vocation sows good seed in that good land that ultimately feeds even the stranger. Judge no one else in their sowing. Neither judge yourself. Some give through family, friendship, and social means. Some give through prayers. Some visit the poor and sick. Others sow seeds of music. Grandparents may sow seeds of giving through their glad tidings, sweet words, and encouragement. Give what you can. Give when and where the Spirit prompts you. The apple seed is unlike the persimmon, yet each holds within itself the wherewithal to feed. So do we: In giving as in life, each of us is called uniquely by the Lord to be a living kernel of abundant good.

Small daily contributions add value to life and expand compassion. Forget legalisms. Raise your standard of giving. This year, tithe 15 percent — not 10 percent. If you've been rude, learn to speak kindly. Function suitably. Concentrate on what's facing you. (Pure focus is pure giving.) Get out of people's way. Get out of your own way. (Life needs room to breathe. *Serve Life.*) Then your day's work will fit like comfortable shoes.

Master, which is the great commandment in the law?
Jesus said unto him, Thou shalt love the Lord thy God with all
thy heart, and with all thy soul, and with all thy mind.
This is the first and great commandment.
And the second is like unto it,
Thou shalt love thy neighbor as thyself. (MATTHEW 22:36–39)

ఆఖఆఖఆఖఆఖఆఖఆఖ

Observing the nuances and practical patterns of your every-
day life, you may wish to reflect on the following questions
(or ones you prefer and create for yourself) during the course
of the week . . .

- Name three special gifts — the "seed" you could invest —
  from which fulfilling service to yourself and others might
  follow *today*. What have others told you that you do well?
  What tasks are easy for you to do well?

- Reviewing the past couple of weeks, what small *daily* contributions do you routinely make? In what ways are these
  acts contributive?

- On a scale of 1 to 10 (10 being the highest), what marks
  do you give yourself as a "cheerful giver"? What *form* do
  your givings most likely take? What form did your giving
  take today? This week?

Progressive, unique unfoldment of Life's activity in us

Every good gift and every perfect gift is from above...

Having a vocation in no way implies we'll reject corporate jobs. It doesn't mean we'll always shun rewards. Far from it. Some great leaders can fulfill their call only through dynamic organizational giving, while other giants of influence can promote our welfare only through prayer, their written word, their hidden sacrificial life.

Just being ourselves gives us much to do along *any* line of endeavor. Cleaning a sink is sacred work when it's done as for the Lord, and not for persons. Investing our full focus in such chores, the tasks at hand predictably reveal more to be and do.

We ourselves *are* the holy work, the work in progress that, when ready, reflects ripe, ineffable love, as well as concrete giving. Remember from whence your good gifts come.

Do not err, my beloved brethren.
Every good gift and every perfect gift is from above,
and cometh down from the Father of lights,
with whom is no variableness, neither shadow of turning.
Of his own will begat he us with the word of truth,
that we should be a kind of firstfruits of his creatures.

(JAMES 1:16–18)

❧❧❧❧❧❧❧

Observing the nuances and practical patterns of your everyday life, you may wish to reflect on the following questions (or ones you prefer and create for yourself) during the course of the week...

❧ As you observe yourself working with others, on what occasions do you lose *self*-consciousness or the desire to curry favor? What elements precede those times? How do you feel before, during, and after such happenings?

❧ In what three or four ways do you currently invest your work with a sort of sacred quality? When is this most likely to occur? When did that occur *today?*

❧ How do you interpret the notion "We ourselves *are* the work in progress"? What words and examples might you use to describe what this phrase means to you as a distinctive individual? How, specifically, were you a work-in-progress today?

Practical skill plus spiritual wisdom

Remember ye not the former things . . .

Without strong faith, it may seem frightful to discover that work which once brought pleasure no longer does. Or that some important chapter of enterprise is ending. Faith trusts what's coming, and the art of giving includes the embrace of pruning. Even ours. If ultimately we bear more fruit, we testify to Love. In truth, there is no end and no beginning, simply the progressive turning of so-called closings into fresh starts. What does this mean for us, *today?*

Intuition, our sudden wish to tackle something untried, may be a spiritual wisdom. By trusting life's deepest mysteries for practical answers we dissolve fictive beliefs: Prayer and the Word of God show us we *can* more forward. Somewhere in consciousness, we already have. In Christ, we ourselves *are* the forward movement, the light that is the life of humankind.

All things and all transitions are made possible if we love God. The Spirit of Love leads us out of seeming dead-ends. Love knows only liberty. The eternal *I am* sets us free.

Remember ye not the former things, neither consider the things
  of old.
Behold, I will do a new thing; now it shall spring forth;
shall ye not know it? I will even make a way in the wilderness,
  and rivers in the desert. . . .
I, even I, am he that blotteth out thy transgressions for mine
  own sake, and will not remember thy sins. (ISAIAH 43:18–25)

Observing the nuances and practical patterns of your every-
day life, you may wish to reflect on the following questions
(or ones you prefer and create for yourself) during the course
of the week . . .

- In your relationships, leisure time, or work in general,
  how would you describe the stuckness (or "dead-end
  ruts") you've experienced today? Lately?

- What aspects of your present life are no longer fulfilling or meaningful? How might you employ your deepest
  mind (imagination, intuition, dream life, etc.) to remedy
  this *today?*

- When, if ever, have you experienced wisdom as "at hand"
  and what might you do to increase the likelihood of that
  happening more frequently?

Love's purposes, reflected in us

Let the beauty of the Lord be upon us . . .

Has Love unfolded fruitfulness? Even a fruitful way of *being* follows mature love — the joyful self-vanishing that bears Love's mark. Who appreciates in advance the extent of what can be done when being flows from intimacy with God? Love makes the least act potent.

Changing a flat tire or a baby's diaper effectively requires discipline and a self-forgetful mind. Love's plan for us includes effectiveness. (Consider those who *say* they love — a child, a home, a project — yet because they lack love are inept, neglectful, even hurtful.)

Love shows us how to walk with, and not against, our tempo, our pace, our inborn timing or given way of meeting goals. Love lets us wait patiently for the righteous opening while we hone skills or save funds for a venture. Rightly handled, waiting *is* prayer, is intimate communion. No matter how full or empty our coffers, *subjectively* we're always "rich" when true to our vocation and "poor" — joyless, frustrated, bitter, victimized, defeated — when betraying it. By injecting a praiseful, truthful love into whatever we do, we become eternity's signature.

Let thy work appear unto thy servants,
and thy glory unto their children.
And let the beauty of the Lord our God be upon us:
and establish thou the work of our hands upon us;
yea, the work of our hands establish thou it.

(PSALM 90:16–17)

ଈ୬ ଈ୬ ଈ୬ ଈ୬ ଈ୬ ଈ୬

Observing the nuances and practical patterns of your every-day life, you may wish to reflect on the following questions (or ones you prefer and create for yourself) during the course of the week...

- What does "fruitfulness" mean to you in your day-to-day initiations and follow-throughs of projects, relationships, circumstances?

- How, specifically, might you inject an *appropriate* authenticity into your efforts this day?

- As you move through today, what inborn or deeply rooted inclinations stimulate your focus, enthusiasm, productive energies, and willing service? How might you use these cues to identify your vocation?

Full engagement, here and now

None of us live to ourselves . . .

The richly occupied are ever hospitable to Love's interior cues, the Spirit abiding within. They demonstrate a right focus. They stick with what's worth doing. By faith they get a pit bull's grip on the divine image dwelling within. The saintly Augustine of Hippo instructed us: "Hold out, be steadfast, endure, bear the delay, and you have carried the cross."[5]

The richly occupied cleave to their visions and dreams. The old adage "To live the thing, dream it first" applies. Mindfully they court the spiritual essence undergirding Creation and thereby loose whatever's good within their dreams. Their "what could be" is, at best, their apprehension of what *is* — their calling of what isn't as though it were. To be sure, such mystical communion can be disruptive. Unsettling. So be it. In this, each vocation is a meandering, inward listening process — not a tidy, isolated feat. Inspired living, spontaneous and true, comes by plugging into the sanctified here and now. Full engagement lets us bear the delay.

For none of us liveth to himself, and no man dieth to himself.
For whether we live, we live unto the Lord;
and whether we die, we die unto the Lord;
whether we live therefore, or die, we are the Lord's.

∞∞∞∞∞∞

Observing the nuances and practical patterns of your every-day life, you may wish to reflect on the following questions (or ones you prefer and create for yourself) during the course of the week . . .

- How do you feel when you are richly and fully engaged? What do you seem to be doing during those times?

- What one or two "dreams of possibility" did you shelve long ago? Why or to what extent do those dreams still linger in your mind and heart?

- To what degree and in what fashion do you commune with your inmost self? Today, what two or three pastimes call forth your dreams or creative process?

"Play for mortal stakes"

The rejected stone
becomes the head stone...

A true vocation utilizes every nuance of mortal experience for immortal purposes. Even supposed loss becomes a gain. In truth, nothing is ever lost.

Despite delays, setbacks, and self-doubt, over time we
conceive fresh possibilities especially as we love and labor
simply — just as ourselves. Rightly apprehended, all gifts,
even the most commonplace, eventually come out of hiding,
meld into one pristine offering subordinated to Love.

By grace, the butcher, the baker, the candlestick maker
transform what's done each day, as Robert Frost wrote,
into "play for mortal stakes ... for Heaven and the future's
sakes."[6]

I will praise thee: for thou hast heard me,
and art become my salvation.
The stone which the builders refused
is become the head stone of the corner.
This is the Lord's doing; it is marvelous in our eyes.
This is the day which the Lord hath made;
we will rejoice and be glad in it.

(PSALM 118:21–24)

&❧&❧&❧&❧&❧&❧

Observing the nuances and practical patterns of your every-day life, you may wish to reflect on the following questions (or ones you prefer and create for yourself) during the course of the week . . .

❧ Recalling any rejected — seemingly lost — aspects of self, what undeveloped traits, aspirations, or relationships still haunt your mind? What does that tell you?

❧ In what ways might old disappointments, loss, delays, and abandoned dreams emerge from *disuse* and become vital threads in the vocational fabric of your life?

❧ Each day this week, how would you complete the following sentence: Today, laboring "just as myself" (in my own pace and manner), I rejoiced in the day by . . .

Movement toward the sacred

Now the parable is this:
the seed is the word of God . . .

How would *you* describe the Word of God? With what language do you tell of your own "spirit"? How do you speak or act your values into being? A vocation stimulates any number of diverse drives to know and reflect an inner life.[7] Religion may comprise a particular and potentially fixed system of beliefs (what with its special rites, organized rituals and vocabulary, and worldview), but spirituality is soft and unfixed — potentially embarrassing — our heart's movement toward the sacred.

What words do you use to explore the ineffable core of your most sacred, virtuous self? Your mystical side? Your subtle sense of the holy, your quest for purpose or meaning?[8] Which of your routine sacrifices — made for, say, family or some important aim — are a seed of conscious willingness to be used up for Love's sake? Be of good cheer. Such seeming sacrifice is spiritual planting, Love's work shining through our work to bear lasting fruit.

And he said, Unto you it is given to know
the mysteries of the kingdom of God:
but to others in parables;
that seeing they might not see,
and hearing they might not understand.
Now the parable is this:
The seed is the word of God.

(LUKE 8:10–11)

∽ჱ∽ჱ∽ჱ∽ჱ∽ჱ∽ჱ

Observing the nuances and practical patterns of your every-day life, you may wish to reflect on the following questions (or ones you prefer and create for yourself) during the course of the week...

∽ How would you describe your spirit?

∽ Spiritually speaking, today what words, fleeting images, sounds, habits, and atmosphere brought *you* to life?

∽ Name at least three routine sacrifices you've made today (i.e., out of love). What resulted emotionally and spiritually as a result of these choices? What did you learn? As you review your week, what do your routine sacrifices tell you about your routine "plantings"?

Honoring Love's spirit

The seed springs forth,
he knoweth not how . . .

A desire for increased competence, an unrelenting wish to honor the deep things of life, incomprehensible inner cues — empathy, longing, despair, or feelings of illogical gratefulness — move us to relinquish worn-out restraints or lethargies for Life's sake. To do that each day, to choose an unbounded existence — the "I Am" and the "Yes, I Can" stance of God — makes us a catalyst not only for ourselves, but also for others. "I set myself on fire," remarked John Wesley, "and people come to watch me burn."[9]

To the vocationally maturing, spiritual sensibilities fuel new, higher standards for that fired-up ascent. Yielding to Love's business in us we find that "our business" is generally a little different from what we'd imagined it would be.

Choosing Life each morning — perhaps by speaking God's word into our life — we use the smallest obstacles wisely, reveal talent and a seed of promise that, bit by bit, blossoms into sheer *being*, the best self we already are. Love's seed is infinitely expansive, supremely intelligent, yet no one knows precisely *how* it works.

And he said, So is the kingdom of God,
as if a man should cast seed into the ground;
And should sleep, and rise night and day,
and the seed should spring and grow up,
he knoweth not how. (MARK 4:26–27)

❧❧❧❧❧❧

Observing the nuances and practical patterns of your every-day life, you may wish to reflect on the following questions (or ones you prefer and create for yourself) during the course of the week . . .

❧ Whom do you know personally with a "high spiritual I.Q."? How would you describe that person's attributes, mode of functioning, or ability to focus and solve problems creatively? How might you describe *your own* spiritual I.Q.?

❧ If, today, you painted a picture of your "wilderness" — the heart-regions beckoning you to further growth and exploration — what might that look like? What colors, images, attitudes, moods, or special feelings would you want to depict?

❧ Today, what precisely might it mean to surrender to Love's business in you? What does "Love's business" entail in terms of your current purposes?

A practical synergy of our finest faculties

*. . . that ye might be filled
with the knowledge of the Lord's will*

However we arrive at it, a vocation is *practical*. It links the inmost self to a constructive way of being in community. Whether we are marketing experts, graphic designers, or refuse haulers, a vocation unleashes unseen spiritual energies that support our tangible success. With a properly focused attention, all occupational outcomes improve: sales results, expansion plans, customer and work relationships. It's never too late.

Have we endured years of insecurity instead of freeing up our vocational truths? Have we been slothful, weak-willed, or befuddled? A blessed illumination changes that. The synergy of our mind's finest faculties results in invisible power — supernatural resources — to be employed in daily life. Faith, prayer, an absolute refusal to place our trust in worldly goods, returns us to true Security: God with us, available — our living fount of water, welling up to substantive wisdom and eternal life.

... desire that ye might be filled
with the knowledge of his will
in all wisdom and spiritual understanding;
That ye might walk worthy of the Lord unto all pleasing,
being fruitful in every good work,
and increasing in the knowledge of God.

(COLOSSIANS 1:9–10)

❧❧❧❧❧❧❧

Observing the nuances and practical patterns of your everyday life, you may wish to reflect on the following questions (or ones you prefer and create for yourself) during the course of the week...

❧ *Today,* what two or three practical faculties might you bring to others?

❧ *Today,* what sort of "unseen energies" furthered your efforts, optimism, kindness, compassion, productivity, etc.? How did that affect others in your sphere (either incidentally or directly)?

❧ On a scale of 1 to 10 (10 being highest), how great is your *willingness* to be filled with "the knowledge of the Lord's will"? What does that phrase mean to you? Using the same scale, how would you rate your *resistance* today to that knowledge? (Consider undergoing the same self-assessment process for faith, prayer, and absolute refusal to place trust in externals, like money.)

Truth-telling

Fear thou not, for I am with you . . .

A re we inwardly secure enough to be just ourselves? Unmasked, speaking the truth — *being* the truth — about what we value and intend? Unmasking is a sacred task for saints and fools alike. Fools tend to hide. Saints are blazingly themselves. Consider St. Francis — thin, quick, poetic, a "live wire," it is said, who listened to angels and birds for inspiration. Compare his mode of being to St. Thomas of Aquinas, called the "dumb ox" for his heavy, placid, plodder's way.[10] Both were bold, blessed truth-tellers, vocationally alive in God.

"Where art thou?" asked God of Adam and Eve, self-consciously hiding from the Lord. "Where art thou?" asks God of *us*. Are we straight-out and unselfconsciously ourselves? Or hiding?

Truth-telling tolerates no compromises, and as such can make us feel naked and exposed. Or it can revive a primordial fear of punishment. Truth-tellers find their vocation by being real; the realities of actual conditions unfold the path. In saint-like (or foolish) fashion, eventually a vocation teaches truth-tellers to love their own unmasking. Mysteriously then truth becomes their sanest, surest response — the ultimate antidote for whatever's ailing life.

Fear thou not; for I am with thee: be not dismayed;
for I am thy God: I will strengthen thee; yea, I will help thee;
yea, I will uphold thee with the right hand of my righteousness.
Behold, all they that were incensed against thee shall be ashamed
and confounded: they shall be as nothing;
and they that strive with thee shall perish. . . .
For I the Lord thy God will hold thy right hand, saying unto
thee, Fear not; I will help thee. (ISAIAH 41:10–13)

᭺᭺᭺᭺᭺᭺

Observing the nuances and practical patterns of your every-day life, you may wish to reflect on the following questions (or ones you prefer and create for yourself) during the course of the week . . .

ᨀ When have you been hurt or discounted by revealing your truths to someone? What lessons did that bring you? What were the costs and consequences of those experiences and how does that guide you today?

ᨀ Has it ever happened that someone who was "incensed against thee" was mistaken, then ashamed? Describe what you learned. Have *you* ever been incensed by some-one you loved only to be ashamed later? Describe what you learned.

ᨀ On the other side of telling (or hiding) your life's truths, what have you discovered about yourself? How might these life lessons affect your work choices?

Faith at work

I can of mine own self do nothing . . .

G rowth toward the high awareness of truth-telling and a true calling requires an active, positive faith. Faith guides us through those tricky meetings with our bullying supervisor or ultra-critical client. Faith prospers us as good ideas lead us to the safe port of leaving well enough alone. Strong faith lets us trust whatever light we're shown this day. That steady, forward movement builds faith as it releases faith. Yet faith does not blindly venture into snares, for God's Word is a light unto its feet.

Sufficient for each day is the wisdom of that day, and a healthy discernment accompanies all trusting movement. Lacking high spiritual intelligence — strong faith, Abraham's faith, intimate oneness with God — we're probably not *ready* to advance.

I can of mine own self do nothing:
as I hear, I judge:
and my judgment is just;
because I seek not mine own will,
but the will of the Father which hath sent me.

(JOHN 5:30)

❧❧❧❧❧❧❧

Observing the nuances and practical patterns of your everyday life, you may wish to reflect on the following questions (or ones you prefer and create for yourself) during the course of the week . . .

❧ When trials come your way, how do you typically cope, and what part does faith play in your response to a crisis or challenge? *Today,* when did you "walk by faith"?

❧ Name at least three times during the week when your faith brought you through the dark. Describe the pattern of those happenings. What does that pattern tell you?

❧ If you were telling a beloved child *how* to cultivate strong faith, what advice might you give? (To what extent have you followed your own advice *today?*)

The sacred melding of heart and reason

Serve the Lord with gladness . . .

A vocation invites a perfect fusion of our finest intellectual forces — rational and seemingly irrational. With less thought to self and more to God, we grow increasingly identified with that call, more capable and, simultaneously, aligned with what's ours to do.

Garnering such inner wealth depends on logical and transcendent processes, on faith in unseen promises and feedback from concrete reality — on worldly and otherworldly wit. (Was this what Aquinas called "the middle way"?) That sacred melding involves our very nature: the fabric of consciousness is oneness, indivisible unity, *living* in the love of God.

To master our craft, service, or profession, we take small and giant steps in growing trust and capability, rejoicing as we learn to manage all our ventures expertly.

Serve the Lord with gladness:
come before his presence with singing.
Know ye that the Lord he is God:
it is he that hath made us, and not we ourselves;
we are his people, and the sheep of his pasture.
Enter into his gate with thanksgiving,
and into his courts with praise:
be thankful unto him, and bless his name.

(PSALM 100:2–4)

⋄⋄⋄⋄⋄⋄⋄

Observing the nuances and practical patterns of your every-day life, you may wish to reflect on the following questions (or ones you prefer and create for yourself) during the course of the week...

⋄ Design a twenty-four-hour period in which you'd fulfill-ingly practice giving "less thought to self and more to God." What three or four new actions might you take? What schedule would you follow? What environment would you enjoy?

⋄ What is the possibility and prudence of actualizing more of that day, say, over the coming weekend or next holiday?

⋄ How much actual rejoicing do you do in an average day? What does a rejoicing nature look and sound like *in* you? In your close friends? Who seems joyful or of a "rejoicing" nature? Describe that person.

Summary: What constitutes vocation?

- Love's inconvenient prod to love,
- Becoming a vital cell in the collective body,
- Subjective affluence,
- An inner call to functional wholeness,
- Increased spiritual intelligence,
- Distinctive service to self and other,
- Progressive, unique unfoldment of Life's activity in us,
- Practical skill plus spiritual wisdom,
- Love's purposes, reflected in us,
- Full engagement, here and now,
- "Play for mortal stakes,"
- Movement toward the sacred,
- Honoring Love's spirit,
- A practical synergy of our finest faculties,
- Truth-telling,
- Faith at work,
- The sacred melding of heart and reason.

Part II

HOW? HEARING VOCATION'S CALL

Rather than scouting for some job in linear, legalistic terms, we listen inwardly. While counselors or professors might well point us in profitable career directions, only the small still voice within seeds an awareness of a sublime function — *something* we can do because of who we are. Volunteering, parenting and other non-salaried efforts are often vocationally inspired. Pure intent, feelings of longing and gratitude precede and accompany a vocational theme of life.

Prayer, meditation on Scripture, daily tasks done in disciplined, self-forgetful service somehow unite us with whatever is authentically ours to do. And this union blesses us. Our work itself, the relationships flowing from it, and our growth into the Lord all favor us supernaturally — if and when our call expresses God's nature, thought, and purposes.

When our work contributes to others (whether we "love" what we're doing or not, whether we articulate our purposes in religious or secular terms), our interior movement gives witness to and cultivates discernment of true vocation. We don't use up or lean exclusively on inborn gifts, but move beyond these. No one this side of eternity can say precisely what that will mean or what Life will require of us.

For where your treasure is, there will your heart be also.
(MATTHEW 6:21)

Be a willing good steward of God's gifts

*There are diversities of gifts,
but the same spirit . . .*

How does Love move us? For some of us the non-remunerative path — like parenting or travel or the Peace Corps — *is* vocation. For others, the visible leadership role is a must. They feel, "Whatever it takes — even if I must assume three jobs — I intend to support my love properly." Then, to repeat an old Persian proverb, they go and wake up their luck.[11]

Our three or four jobs, whether menial or grand, are merely steps taken to cross new thresholds of responsibility. We wait on tables, drive trucks, or join fancy accounting firms while hammering out the details of our calling. Our vocation is *in* us before it's evident in our world. Whatever we are summoned to do, our deepest contribution comes from intimate oneness with God. Being willing, good stewards of God's gifts comes by asking ourselves, "What might a stewardly willingness require of me today?"

Now there are diversities of gifts, but the same Spirit.

And there are differences of administrations, but the same Lord.

And there are diversities of operations, but it is the same God which worketh all in all.

But the manifestations of the Spirit is given to every man to profit withal. (1 CORINTHIANS 12:4–7)

For the next week, consider completing an observational exercise like the following in your private journal or spiritual diary . . .

- Every night, before retiring, jot down three times during the day when you've been a *willing, good steward* of God's gifts and list the gifts involved.

- Every night, before retiring, jot down three times during the day when you've not been a willing, good steward of God's gifts, and list the resistances you've used.

- At week's end, review your notes. What do your patterns of response say to you?

- Might repeating this sort of exercise all month have value for you?

Improve the small details and choices of everyday life

Faithful in that which is least,
we are faithful in much . . .

W hat happens to our productive zest during lackluster days? Do we function, even then? Good calls to good: Working from the heart lets us sow thankful deeds for what we can do, and are offered to do, *today* — no matter what it is. Brother Lawrence scrubbed pots for the love of God. When he was done he prayed. He had one simple rule: Just use whatever is done to commune intimately with the Lord. Our Friend is always near, closer to us than our breath.[12] All creaturely ideas of success, all human notions of security essentially mislead.

A vocation aims to return us to infinite Life. Fidelity matters — how loyally we approach the day. We can assess ourselves: Do we suppress our truths? Or release them with courage? Here Albert Camus can guide us: "To know oneself one should assert oneself."[13] Do we know, and do we say what we mean? Small, authentic choices complete us uniquely — not because of *our* efforts (lest anyone should boast) but because, even in our dry, confusing season, Life waters its own seed of faithfulness in us.

He that is faithful in that which is least is faithful also in much: and he that is unjust in the least is unjust also in much.
If therefore ye have not been faithful in the unrighteous mammon, who will commit to your trust the true riches? (LUKE 16:10–11)

For the next week, consider completing an observational exercise like the following in your private journal or spiritual diary . . .

- At day's end this week review those times you "worked from the heart" *each* day, and describe what that behavior entailed: how you felt; what you discovered; what feedback you received; what you learned. How *faithful* to that which is least were you?

- At the end of the week, review your notes. What do your own patterns of faithfulness or resistance say to you?

- Would repeating this sort of exercise all month have value for you?

Build functional fitness

We were bought with a price . . .

Have we chosen well? Are our purposes and themes of life at least occasionally lucid? Contrast the befuddlement of people who don't know what they want out of life to the clarity of those who are somehow secure with their aims, who love the Lord before all else, and whose work is both play and prayer, both vocation and invocation.

Obeying an expansive inner summons we'll feel lifted out of ourselves and say, "I'd pay to do this," or "I can't believe I'm earning money doing this!"

Settle yourself once and for all. You are no longer your own. Let go. *Choose* to yield to your soul's longing, your call to functional fitness and mastery of some sort. No matter what your lot, do what you love — enjoy, respect, trust, value, hold sacred — with moment-to-moment competence. Mastery begets mastery. Start now. Start small. Do what's possible today with your freedoms of choice. Be reliable. For Life's joy is your strength, and that joy liberates you.

Let every man abide in the same calling wherein he was called.
Art thou called being a servant?
Care not for it; but if thou mayest be made free, use it rather.
For he that is called in the Lord, being a servant, is the Lord's
    freeman:
likewise also he that is called, being free, is Christ's servant.
Ye are bought with a price; be not ye the servants of men.

(1 CORINTHIANS 7:20–23)

❧❧❧❧❧❧

For the next week, consider completing an observational exercise like the following in your private journal or spiritual diary ...

❧ Before you begin working today, note (to yourself) what you want to accomplish this day. Write a general statement of intent *every* morning and list two or three *specific* goals. Each evening, before retiring, note your results. To what extent did your daily conduct and goals reflect the "joy of the Lord"? What criteria are you using for your observation and evaluation?

Today's general intent:

Two or three specific goals:

Results that reflected "the joy of the Lord":

Be Love's touch, constructively

Do good to them that hate you . . .

Do we consider our tasks through a filter of what we value (not what we think we *should* value)? Resentful dutifulness is not born of love. False striving is not born of Love. Bondage keeps us low and sorry — chained to wrong masters, sad circumstances, in need of supports and external prods. And mad. As Love illumines our path, slavish perspectives dissolve.

Choose to do what you must do. Whether you wash dishes or prepare financial reports, let Love be your reason and your shine. Celebrate this day with kind, gentle words and a right focus. Make lovely some small space of your cosmos: Order your desk? Your window garden? Your junk drawer? Open doors for others? Share umbrellas in the rain?

Be Love's touch appropriately, constructively — at home, on the highway, in business. Encourage others quietly and watch what happens.

For we are labourers together with God:
ye are God's husbandry, ye are God's building.
According to the grace of God which is given unto me,
as a wise masterbuilder,
I have laid the foundation, and another buildeth thereon.
But let every man take heed how he buildeth thereupon.

(1 CORINTHIANS 3:9–10)

ക്ക-ക്ക-ക്ക-ക്ക-ക്ക-ക്ക

For the next week, consider completing an observational exercise like the following in your private journal or spiritual diary . . .

❧ For one week, each night before you retire, name three things to which you brought beauty, order, or "Love's touch" — constructively. To what degree were you self-forgetting or working with abandon during such moments? How appropriate and adroit were you? What do your observations tell you?

Accept leadership over whatever needs doing

*Whatsoever good thing we do,
the same shall we receive . . .*

Have we accepted leadership over our lives? That ability and influence is spiritual in the main. Conditions may require us to tackle seemingly inauthentic or tedious jobs, yet with positive self-leadership our motives for accepting such work become purely our own. Perhaps we've always wanted to be a landscaper but blamed our lack of follow-through on insecurity. Let us think again, bolster ourselves inwardly, build faith, release our "I can" power.

To be released, talent must be buttressed by spiritual strength — transcendent, restorative power. Let us renew our minds in God. Rather then trying to "do" that, we can *be* it, allow our intrinsic call to do *us,* to flow through us. Only good ground bears such fruit. What renewing thoughts are we sowing in our ground of being? It helps to have an occasional talk with someone we trust, someone whose own life evidences mastery, the poise and purposes of a true vocation.

Influencing ourselves toward a well-lived life *is* progress. Submitting to the integrity of whatever needs doing is progress. With easy determination, let's become *fit* enough to express whatever is of value that's ours to share.

With good will doing service, as to the Lord, and not to men:
Knowing that whatsoever good thing any man doeth,
the same shall he receive of the Lord, whether he be bond or free.

(EPHESIANS 6:7–8)

❧❧❧❧❧❧

For the next week, consider completing an observational exercise like the following in your private journal or spiritual diary . . .

❧ Before retiring, list something you enjoyed doing today that reflected your responsible, successful leadership (i.e., influence over yourself and/or others), compassionate service, kindness, love of beauty, etc.

❧ To what degree were you self-forgetting or working with abandon during these times, and what, at week's end, do your observations tell you about your ability — or willingness — to accept leadership over what needs doing?

Cultivate the muscles of an active Love

Let us be gentle, patient unto all . . .

I f we *don't* love our job, then at least let's set ourselves toward it in loving service to God. "We ought not be weary of doing little things for the love of God, who regards not the greatness of the work, but the love with which it is performed," advised Brother Lawrence.[14] We can answer the phone politely, send out those papers promptly, give the complainer in our midst an extra ounce of time. Service as spiritual discipline transforms each effort into a lavish experience. "Serving" means adding value, not being slavish, not being abused. We are the Lord's servant, not the world's. Firm gentleness or patience unites us with God — not the world. When we "go the extra mile" today, let us remember who's beside us.

To the extent any activity sanctifies Life, *we* are infused with energetic purpose. Life's rule commands: Give generously and find yourself favored. Give as you can, not as you can't. Love as you can, not as you can't. A vocation builds up the muscles of an active, honest generosity. Then Life itself rewards us with new confidence.

Study to show thyself approved unto God,
a workman that needeth not to be ashamed,
rightly dividing the word of truth . . .
And the servant of the Lord must not strive;
but be gentle unto all men, apt to teach, patient . . .

(2 TIMOTHY 2:15, 24)

∽✧∽✧∽✧∽✧∽✧∽✧

For the next week, consider completing an observational exercise like the following in your private journal or spiritual diary . . .

- Before retiring, list *three* tangible ways in which you *enjoyed* adding value to others (and/or yourself) this day. Describe your manner or mode of receiving enjoyment — how did you experience joy?

- List at least *one* time today when your gentleness, joy, patience, or helpfulness improved some circumstance. What do your week's-end summaries and observations tell you?

Walk the talk productively, and in faith

By works our faith is made perfect...

C an we say "yes" and "no" as if we mean it? Even to ourselves? Do we trust our own word in most matters? Ultimately a vocation asks us to demonstrate our high ideals and standards. Whether we're chopping onions in the kitchen or giving a speech in the boardroom, let's execute our tasks flawlessly, with discipline, imagination, and constructive follow-through.

A vocation moves us beyond the paying of mere lip-service to what's elegant or forgiving. We walk our talk. We decline lesser engagements for what we sense is greater: the best use of time, the meaningful encounter. Just because we're serving the Lord does not mean we're to be passive. Rather, we know the spiritual side of work is, in everyday terms, frequently grubby. Tasks and people are demanding, often intrusive. Whatever else it is, a vocation is also *real*. The choices that structure a strong, righteous faith speak loudest of all and can irritate others. Who grows into a perfect faith without a trial or two? Who learns what faith can accomplish without consciously, judiciously acting on that faith? Practice makes perfect.

Was not Abraham our father justified by works,
when he had offered Isaac his son upon the altar?
Seest thou how faith wrought with his works,
and by works was faith made perfect?

(JAMES 2:21–22)

❧ ❧ ❧ ❧ ❧ ❧

For the next week, consider completing an observational exercise like the following in your private journal or spiritual diary . . .

❧ Before retiring, describe a time today when you executed some task or plan in a flawless, faithful, timely fashion (i.e., effectively and with loyal precision). How did you feel? To what extent did that act hone your faith? At the end of this week, review your notes. What do your observations tell you?

Complete small, seemingly insignificant things well

Hold fast to confidence
which has great recompense of reward . . .

L ife loves competence. Effectiveness is growth's sidekick.
Creating work we love asks us to *do* well those things,
small and large, that actualize our spiritual capability and
wholeness. One moment begs us to control our temper. The
next demands we bring fear under foot. Self-respect surges
each time we complete so-called minor intentions expertly:
pay bills on time, ask for a raise adroitly, put intruders in
their place. Consider David's poise when he did battle with
the Philistine, holding his own with five smooth stones and
a faith that said the battle was the Lord's (see 1 Sam. 17:
32–58).

This holding of one's own is rarely automatic. Such conduct often rubs against the reasoned grain of entrenched
habits, over-politeness, what others expect. That might ex-
plain why those who follow a vocation seem spiritually heroic.
Like a young David — or a Mother Teresa or a Julian of
Norwich — those who step out competently toward their diverse Goliath goals know that faith requires corresponding
acts and trust the Lord for confidence.

Cast not away therefore your confidence,
which hath great recompense of reward.
For ye have need of patience,
that, after ye have done the will of God,
ye might receive the promise.

(HEBREWS 10:35–36)

––––––

For the next week, consider completing an observational exercise like the following in your private journal or spiritual diary . . .

– Before retiring each day this week, name one thing you completed *enjoyably* today that furthered your own spiritual self-realization. Name one thing you didn't enjoy that furthered you. Describe the measures or standards you are using to evaluate your "furtherance." At the end of the week, what does your pattern of reflective comments reveal?

Meditate on functional wholeness as available and at hand

*The Spirit itself bears witness
with our spirit . . .*

To what extent do you believe in spiritual wholeness? Reflect on that phrase for awhile: What does it mean to you? Faith in spiritual wholeness is one key to vocation. How can we travel to a land, or enter and occupy its territory without a conviction that it exists? What does the injunction "Be ye holy, for I am holy" (1 Pet. 1:16) imply to *you?*

Consider taking a short moratorium to ponder your life's wholeness. What would that state of being — or "holy work" — require of you or look like? A spiritual retreat, a hiking adventure, contemplative prayer, a week at the lake clears the mind.

Do you trust or do you doubt your call to spiritual wholeness? In the Spirit, all healing — that is to say, wholeness — is at hand.

For ye have not received the spirit of bondage again to fear;
but ye have received the Spirit of adoption,
whereby we cry, Abba, Father.
The Spirit itself beareth witness with our spirit,
that we are the children of God. . . . (ROMANS 8:15–16)

⊷⊷⊷⊷⊷⊷

For the next week, consider completing an observational exercise like the following in your private journal or spiritual diary . . .

⊷ Today before retiring — or in your early morning hours — visualize, then note in your journal, five upcoming activities that have the potential to enhance you spiritually. At the end of the week, select at least one such activity that you'd like to begin next week.

Bless Life by heeding Life

Thine ears shall hear a word . . .

Are we able — are we willing — to sit absolutely still for just a few minutes each day? Are we able — are we willing — to chew on a verse or two of Scripture each day, to ingest that living food before all else? From perfect stillness comes perfect truth, as Isaiah put it, "a word behind thee." An original idea, an awareness of opportunity, a revelation of having been mistaken and the corresponding wish to apologize, reach out, or accommodate someone — these "words" point us to ourselves as holy work: We are the living, lively stones building up God's house: "Be ye holy . . ."

Vocation's strategic vision — how to do this or that — comes by reflecting on God's Word. Divine guidance, not our own cunning, and innocent trust in God's Word seed spiritual intelligence, the timely, surprising wisdom that baffles even us.

And thine ears shall hear a word behind thee, saying,
This is the way, walk ye in it,
when ye turn to the right hand,
and when ye turn to the left. (ISAIAH 30:21)

❧❧❧❧❧❧

For the next week, consider completing an observational exercise like the following in your private journal or spiritual diary . . .

❧ Consider sitting quietly for just five minutes each day, after awakening. Review the passage above from Isaiah as you sit. Notice whatever you experience. Write down a sentence or two that describes today's sitting experience.

At the end of this week, review your week's remarks and write down a line or two describing whatever your pattern of comments reveals.

Engage in prayer and transcendent daydreaming

Think on whatsoever is pure...

S imple *being* increases spiritual sight, an optimal intelligence of possibilities. Take time to *be* and become brighter. Walk through a forest and become lighter. Meditate on one line of one short psalm and become more hopeful or more insightful than before. Shift your sights upward — to any bit of loveliness — and be adorned by that. At stop lights and cashier stands, practice the art of waiting appreciatively and be uplifted. Isn't Life itself coursing through your veins as you wait?

Children want to get "There" quickly. Patience is, in a sense, supernatural, one fruit of a mature, well-developed heart. In most matters, the less we rush, the better. The less we rush others — or feel them hurrying us — the better. Relax into who and what you are. Relax into the arms of this moment. This, too, is vocation: The praiseful inhaling of Life as it is right now. Enjoy John Muir's words that suggest how most answers come: "So-called sentimental, transcendental dreaming seems the only sensible and substantial business that one can engage in."[15]

Rejoice in the Lord alway; and again I say, Rejoice . . .
Finally, brethren, whatsoever things are true,
whatsoever things are honest,
whatsoever things are just,
whatsoever things are pure,
whatsoever things are lovely,
whatsoever things are of good report:
if there be any virtue, and if there be any praise,
think on these things. (PHILIPPIANS 4:4, 8)

❧❧❧❧❧❧

For the next week, consider completing an observational exercise like the following in your private journal or spiritual
diary . . .

❧ Consider continuing your five minutes of daily quiet
sitting, and now — after that — add *two minutes* of reflection on a line of a psalm or a scriptural passage of your
choice that's meaningful to you. Notice, then describe,
your experience, particularly the effect of your reflection
on the rest of your day. At week's end, review your remarks and write out a line or two describing what the
reflective exercise taught you.

Exploit delays and expect a gradual seasoning of character

*All things work together for good
to those who love God...*

Do you imagine you can *leap* from a survival, materialistic mentality into the supernatural grace of a vocation? Think again. Expect to take some time.

Even Saul — who became Paul when touched by God, "as a light from heaven flashed" (Acts 9:3–4) — underwent a lengthy spiritual seasoning during which his leadership ripened into sheer genius.

So too in the fullness of time are we brought out of our fretful bondage to earthly masters and schedules. At God's pace and appointed time we reach our special genius, our heart's good and rightful place.

And we know that all things work together for good to them that love God,
to them who are the called according to his purpose.

(ROMANS 8:28)

For the next week, consider completing an observational exercise like the following in your private journal or spiritual diary...

- Before retiring this evening, review your day and jot down one event, interpersonal exchange, or experience with potential to "ripen" your leadership abilities.

  How *might* you have used, changed, received, or improved the experience, or your response to it? How *did* you use it? At week's end, what do the patterns of your observations tell you?

Develop the wisdom that confounds the wise

With all thy getting get understanding . . .

Do you crave the quick fix and the instant answer? Get over it. No parent, no teacher, no generous mentor can tell you *precisely* how to discover a fulfilling vocation. Learn to listen inwardly. The treasure hidden within our hearts is far, far above everyone else's (usually trivialized) idea of gainful employment.

The joy of a vocation arrives as we bless Life and become a blessing *to* Life. Learn how to pray, how — and why — to turn to Scripture for guidance, in your own way and time. Remember that, as Mark Twain once said, we cannot pray a lie.[16] Prayer reveals our own truths, leads us into communion with God.

Knowing what "becoming a blessing to Life" means in practical terms is no academic exercise. Wisdom comes by heeding the Holy Spirit. What does that phrase suggest to *you?* That high, bright insight is no mere concept. The living Spirit awaits intelligent, faithful release.

Whatever you're given to do today, follow the Spirit of Truth within as Life leads you to the answers you seek.

Wisdom is the principal thing; therefore get wisdom:
and with all thy getting get understanding.
Exalt her, and she shall promote thee:
she shall bring thee to honour, when thou dost embrace her.
She shall give to thine head an ornament of grace:
a crown of glory shall she deliver to thee. (PROVERBS 4:7–9)

◌◌◌◌◌◌

For the next week, consider completing an observational exercise like the following in your private journal or spiritual diary . . .

- Before retiring, review your day at work, or with family and friends, or while running errands. Describe one time during this day when you *chose* to be a blessing to someone or to some circumstance. How did you feel afterwards? What prompted your decision?

  What skills, attitudes, or response style did you draw on to be a blessing? At week's end, review your remarks and describe what, if anything, your observations tell you.

Summary: How might we hear vocation's call?

- Be a willing good steward of God's gifts,

- Improve the small details and choices of everyday life,

- Build functional fitness,

- Be Love's touch, constructively,

- Accept leadership over whatever needs doing,

- Cultivate the muscles of an active Love,

- Walk the talk productively, and in faith,

- Complete small, seemingly insignificant things well,

- Meditate on functional wholeness as available and at hand,

- Bless Life by heeding Life,

- Engage in prayer and transcendent daydreaming,

- Exploit delays and expect a gradual seasoning of character,

- Develop the wisdom that confounds the wise.

Part III

WHY BOTHER? THE BLESSINGS OF A VOCATION

T he comings and goings of daily life bless us variously. Even we who aren't traditionally devout, yet who follow our natural, creaturely talents, receive subjective rewards from our work. We look forward to certain projects or team meetings. We are stimulated by intellectual exchanges. Our efforts help us forget our cares — and ourselves — and, ultimately, bear fruit. We and those around us are productively furthered.

How much greater then are the blessings bestowed on those of us who consciously affirm a heartfelt call: The more love we express, the more love we receive. That love evidences God. No minor miracle.

As it is written, "Whoever lives in love, lives in God and God in him" (1 John 4:16). The point is that *we* are the holy work we seek. That is our greatest blessing.

> *. . . ye are God's husbandry, ye are God's building.*
> (1 CORINTHIANS 3:9)

We let go of old business and it kisses us goodbye

What have we exchanged for our soul?

Make no mistake: Following a vocation obliges us to relinquish some loves, some supposed securities. We may leave our posh physician's job for desktop graphics work conducted at our kitchen table. We may retire early, while still in our prime. Eventually we'll let go of old business. Or old routines and comforts will kiss *us* goodbye. Never fear: All good comes from Above, from Love's activity in our affairs — and in our mind and heart as well.

Grieve the sad goodbye and get on with Life. Learn to trust Love's bounty. The blessed among us sense Love is all around them. They see all so-called loss as gain.

For whosoever will save his life shall lose it;
but whosoever shall lose his life for my sake and the gospel's, the
same shall save it.
For what shall it profit a man, if he shall gain the whole world,
and lose his soul?
Or what shall a man give in exchange for his soul? (MARK 8:35–37)

✌ ✌ ✌ ✌ ✌ ✌ ✌

Each day for the next week, reflect on what you *have* by considering a question or two along the following lines...

✌ What old routines or "old business" seem to be waning from your ground of being?

✌ Name one new vision, dream, and at least three new images of work that spark your interest these days. *Today?*

✌ Considering *this day,* for what noticeable bounty — no matter how insignificant — are you thankful? At the end of each day this week, list seven such items. At the end of the week, reflect on your entire list.

We make time for Beauty

Let us worship the Lord
in the beauty of holiness . . .

Avocation employs our inner artist fully by awakening the appreciator within. Each morning can call up a new vision of possibilities (and the resulting goals these trigger). Surprisingly, we want to do whatever truly matters — especially in the spring: ride a blue bike with our grandchild, construct a new arbor for our pink vine rose. The more time we reserve for grateful reflection and easy daydreaming, the more inner stillness we gain. This is one bonus of the artist's way: we talk with, and express, our own aesthetic.

A deepened awareness appreciates Beauty, Truth, gray dawns and rose sunsets, an infant's touch. We feel an impulse to view all loveliness as bearing our Maker's mark and now, somehow, tangibly we infuse that new reverence into every day.

O worship the Lord in the beauty of holiness:
fear before him, all the earth. . . .
Let the heavens rejoice, and let the earth be glad;
let the sea roar, and the fullness thereof.
Let the field be joyful, and all that is therein:
then shall all the trees of the wood rejoice.

(PSALM 96:9–12)

❧❧❧❧❧❧

Each day for the next week, reflect on what you *have* by considering a question or two along the following lines . . .

- Reflecting on *this day*, what beauty or symmetry did you appreciate? How did you register or *demonstrate* your appreciation?

- Reflecting on your use of time *this day*, how many minutes or hours did you devote to the simple, prayerful thought, the easy daydream? How might you expand that time tomorrow? What value might that expansion bring?

- Thinking about *this day*, specifically how did — or might — you inject a fresh reverence into your thought-life, friendships, work, or leisure activities? What value do you suppose reverence would bring? What value might you gain out of repeating this exercise all month? All year?

Darkness departs

*Let us not fellowship
with the unfruitful works of darkness . . .*

Whatever grief we're holding on to ultimately lifts. Old hurts or losses dissolve in love. A friend noted, "Pain comes to pass — in order to teach us its lessons and evaporate into nothingness." Forgiveness in love is spontaneous. As our heart opens even to those who have wounded us, forgiveness in love is spontaneous, yet does not necessarily imply fellowship. Still, we feel reshaped by eternity and eventually admit, "I wonder why it took so long for the light to come on." That suggests *years* may pass before we can articulate our feelings of what's truly happening, as forgiveness, in and around us.

A vocation frees us in that reconcilatory way. Its essential stillness transforms us. What begins as a Sunday hobby becomes our radical, distinctive turning toward Creation. We are, in this, like buds seeking out the sun. Warmed by the subtlest harmony, we no longer feel a need to hide or justify disrupting the status quo. Called out of gloom, we head for the neighborhood theater to paint scenery. Or we drive out West to enroll in a school for clowns. Light exists *in* us before it shines through us as "work." As love bears its own fruit, we'll leave whatever's dark or unloving — as well we should. And must.

And have no fellowship with the unfruitful works of darkness,
but rather reprove them. . . .
But all things that are reproved are made manifest by the light:
for whatsoever doth make manifest is light.
Wherefore he saith, Awake thou that sleepest,
and arise from the dead, and Christ shall give thee light.

(EPHESIANS 5:11–14)

✺✺✺✺✺✺

Each day for the next week, reflect on what you *have* by considering a question or two along the following lines . . .

- ✺ Today, as you observe your habitual routines and relationships, what (or who) still draws you into "darkness"? What's your role in — and contribution to — that gloom?

- ✺ Observing yourself *this day*, look for and describe the times, situations, and relationships during which "light exists" most vividly in you.

- ✺ At week's end, review the patterns of your experience. What do you conclude?

We accommodate eternity's plans

Thy years have no end . . .

Naively, we may have expected our creative joys to arrive instantly, like chili dogs at a fast food joint. Or we chase success and find ourselves spinning in circles. "I've been on a career treadmill," observed one man, "running faster and faster, but getting nowhere." Whether we're shaping a piece of clay or a business plan, a vocation shapes *us*, by revealing the distinctive rules of our *own* inventive process. What does that phrase suggest to you? At your best, how do you solve problems?

Some people quietly think their solutions into being. Others brainstorm out loud with a group to *hear* what's on their mind. A vocation holds our answers, our creative archetypes, our right timing and rhythms of expressive salvation.

Let us willingly accept our snail's-pace progress or abrupt zig-zags of regression. Sometimes our consistency is a boon. Sometimes it's a curse. When in doubt, we'll dance with the moment. Or stand and wait. Whatever's holy is timeless, so what's the rush? As we renounce impatience in favor of eternity's plans, we'll relax into the essence of what we are.

Of old hast thou laid the foundation of the earth:
and the heavens are the work of thy hands.
They shall perish, but thou shalt endure:
yea, all of them shall wax old like a garment;
as a vesture shalt thou change them, and they shall be changed:
But thou art the same, and thy years have no end.
The children of thy servants shall continue,
and their seed shall be established before thee. (PSALM 102:25–28)

❧❧❧❧❧❧

Each day for the next week, reflect on what you *have* by considering a question or two along the following lines . . .

❧ Reflecting back on your life to date, when have delays served your highest purposes and best interests? List as many experiences as you can remember, along the following lines:

My goal was . . .	A delay occurred when . . .	Improved outcomes happened when . . .
•	•	•
•	•	•
•	•	•
•	•	•
•	•	•

❧ Reviewing the pattern of your experience, what do you deduce about the wisdom of waiting?

Now we stand in shining light

I will turn away your captivity . . .

The journey from a fearful life to one that's secure and generous moves gradually and largely by faith. A vocation's worshipful tasks draw us into the light of spiritual power. Truth moves *through* us to infuse word and deed with meaning. Said one homemaker, "The more I submitted to my wholesome drives, the more my inborn gifts fulfilled me. Soon, an afternoon of simple baking was one of the most exhilarating ways to spend time."

Our spiritual intelligence — more lavish than a linear, well-reasoned mind — liberates us. Initially, it can seem baffling and inconvenient to listen inwardly, to *try* to hear what, in us, wants expression. Divinely guided, we're aware of unfathomable joy, paths we've overlooked or underestimated. Trusting God honors God and draws down great graces.[17] Trust does not seek blueprints for this communion, yet prayerful faith makes safe the way.

For I know the thoughts I think toward you, saith the Lord,
thoughts of peace, and not of evil, to give you an expected end.
Then shall ye call upon me . . . and I will harken unto you.
And ye shall seek me, and find me,
when ye shall search for me with all your heart.
And I will be found of you, saith the Lord:
and I will turn away your captivity. . . . (JEREMIAH 29:11–14)

⋘⋙⋘⋙⋘⋙

Each day for the next week, reflect on what you *have* by considering a question or two along the following lines . . .

- Considering your life's current, "unsettled," or open-ended issues, what precisely *are* your questions about your vocation? That is, if you were talking to God, how would you articulate your vocational questions? As you read over your favorite lines of Scripture, what do you suppose God's answers would be?

- Approximately how long have you been waiting for answers to your questions?

- What is your usual mode (or state) of being for listening to (or discerning) answers?

- How might you improve your receptivity to your inmost spiritual cues?

We gain our life

And I will restore to you
the years that the locusts hath eaten . . .

E ven when wrapped up in secular or prosaic forms, every vocation affirms Life. According to Voltaire, it spares us from three great evils: boredom, vice, and need. A regained vitality proves we've found our way. "Caring for other people's gardens," noted a landscaper, "helps *me*. I live my cherished values and develop an inner aesthetic, without precisely knowing how. I'm energized just by doing the work well." So do our rough edges smooth out in the light of a redirected attention.

Trusting God for solutions brings them. One person fights for social justice through volunteer work, thereby gaining into a vocation of giving. Patiently, each day she attends to others with diligence. Another might opt for life in a monastery, "called more especially to know the loneliness and cost of the return to holiness," as Gilbert Shaw puts it.[18] Yet a third retires at forty — prematurely it seems — to start a new career of fly-fishing, sensing that the river will bear fruits of a new sort. Thirst to express the gift, longing to develop it — not idealized pictures of self-glory or inordinate self-will — restore the lost years.

Fear not, O land; be glad and rejoice:
for the Lord will do great things.
Be not afraid, ye beasts of the field:
for the pastures of the wilderness do spring,
for the tree beareth her fruit,
the fig tree and the vine do yield their strength . . .
And the floors shall be full of wheat,
and the vats shall overflow with wine and oil.
And I will restore to you
the years that the locusts hath eaten . . .

(JOEL 2:21–25)

એ⊷એ⊷એ⊷એ⊷એ⊷એ

Each day for the next week, reflect on what you *have* by considering a question or two along the following lines . . .

⊷ What thoughts, work, or activities spare you from "boredom, vice, and need"?

⊷ How frequently do you engage in such gainful employment, and in what one area might you add to that engagement *today*?

⊷ What thought pattern or activity tells you you're *gaining* an enhanced life — more vigor, greater insight? If answers to such questions are elusive, if you've never paid attention to such matters before, to what or to whom might you turn for a productive lead or a trusting conversation?

We sing a true song

My glory I will not give to another . . .

Avocation lets us know and *be* ourselves. All authentic service to self and other is sacred, based on an intimate interior relationship. Whether we are young, old, or in between, our heartfelt activities make a joyful noise unto the Lord. Helen Keller said that unless she turned her own glad thoughts into practical living she could not reap a kernel of good.

Like Keller, universally, our wisest mentors guide us back to our own song, to our glad thoughts, our *own* way of practical living that we may honor it. *The Odyssey, Heidi,* the Parable of the Unjust Steward (Luke 16), all enduring art, poetry or film teach one lasting rule: Rejoice in who you really are.

In calm, quiet corners of our gardens, in college classrooms and busy shopping malls, genuineness — Truth — strikes the glad note in Life's glorious refrain.

I am the Lord: that is my name:
and my glory will I not give to another,
neither my praise to graven images.
Behold, the former things are come to pass,
and new things do I declare:
before they spring forth I tell you of them.
Sing unto the Lord a new song,
and his praise from the end of the earth,
ye that go down to the sea, and all that is therein:
the isles, and the inhabitants thereof.

(ISAIAH 42:8–10)

⊱⊰ ⊱⊰ ⊱⊰ ⊱⊰ ⊱⊰ ⊱⊰

Each day for the next week, reflect on what you *have* by considering a question or two along the following lines . . .

⊰ Given what you expect *today* — from your present obligations and schedule — how might you turn *one* of your own glad thoughts into "practical living"? List how you might transform two specific tasks for the better with your glad thoughts.

⊰ What are some new things that seem to spring forth as you reflect on the inquiry above?

We develop a perceptive faith

Through faith we understand...

Strong faith restores us. Faith is the *substance* of desired things. It's the actual heart of the matter. Through faith we understand not just ourselves, but also the very structure of unseen things — what is not yet, but by faith, what is already and has always been. Faith rids our mind of ghosts. It fills old, worn-out vessels with fresh wine, renewed life, revived dreams. An artist observed, "I quit a corporate legal job to design advertising logos, taking on day work at a construction site to pay the bills. My wife supported me for five years. We taught ourselves to live on one salary. Hers. Today, I'm earning enough so that she can quit. We had the common sense — and the faith — to live our dream, and that made all the difference."

Investing in a vocation, we reap heaven's rewards. Good friendships, a sturdy hearth and home, jars of clover honey on our pantry shelves are but sweet reminders of God's omnipresent love.

Through faith we understand that the worlds were framed by the
word of God,
so that things which are seen were not made of things which do
appear. (HEBREWS 11:3)

Each day for the next week, reflect on what you *have* by considering a question or two along the following lines...

- Comparing your current aspirations to your responsibilities, how do you interpret the phrase "perceptive faith"? What in your life has been the difference between strong faith and presumption or impulsivity?

- Considering today's cobwebs of your unproductive or habitual way of thinking, what sort of faith is needed before you kiss these "old ghosts" goodbye once and for all?

- To what trusted counselor or friend might you turn to discuss your faith, the reviving of lost dreams, and your wholesome renewal of life?

We use trials as stepping stones

Nothing from without defiles...

Sometimes a crisis throws us a curve ball before we know how to catch it. This is not all bad: Each challenge is, in every sense, spiritual. Certainly we wonder: "Can I survive this? Can I really cross this bridge?" With faith and practice, we learn to field surprises expertly.

Seeming trials are teachers. They can show us how to break our chains of limits. As we forge a business path in a harrowing global wilderness or apply ourselves artfully to what, at first, feels like drudge work, we build initiative, courage, and an intention to endure. Such attributes are inner resources to be used during trials as stepping stones to strong faith. When we're right *within,* we reign in life — and find out what we're made of in the process.

And when he had called all the people unto him,
he said unto them,
Harken unto me every one of you, and understand:
There is nothing from without a man,
that entering into him can defile him:
but the things which come out of him,
those are they that defile the man.
If any man have ears to hear, let him hear.

(MARK 7:14–16)

❧❧❧❧❧❧

Each day for the next week, reflect on what you *have* by considering a question or two along the following lines . . .

❧ Describe a crisis you met before you were prepared for it. To handle it, what skills and inner resources did you lean on? (Perhaps you located the right mentor to help you through some childhood trauma; perhaps you used insight or your research acumen to locate other answers you needed. In this exercise reflect on your skills, virtues, and solution-finding prowess.) Try to list different inner resources each day.

❧ Given the so-called drudge tasks facing you today (e.g., the filing, washing of floors, car repairing, or grocery shopping), describe — or mentally rehearse — how you might use two of these as "stepping stones" to your best self. At the end of each day, describe in your journal (or mentally evaluate) how you actually handled the tedium of the day.

We know how to rest

We cease from our own works . . .

Life generally happens while we're busy doing something else. Riding the bus to one spot, we detour to another and meet a special friend — the love of our life, perhaps — during the delay. We wrestle effectively with today's book-keeping mess, and tomorrow's finances fall into place. Our encounter with Reality (not how we think things should be) leads us toward a cherished calm. Somehow our daily happenings unfold God's plan, and this is enough to let us rest.

What we *imagine* we're meant to do could turn out (on the long side of experience) to be unlike anything we now expect. We might buy an antique shop while on vacation, or invest in a small-town newspaper on a whim and watch it evolve into a hearty family business. Anything good can happen. "As soon as my head hits the pillow at night," said one book dealer, "I fall asleep. All my problems aren't solved, but I've given the day my best shot and figure that's enough fretting until tomorrow. If something's troubling me, I think to myself, 'I let the peace of God rule in my heart, and I refuse to worry about anything'" (Col. 3:15). To engage wholeheartedly with what's pressing now is to invite eventual harmony. To rest well, love God well.

There remaineth therefore a rest to the people of God.
For he that is entered into his rest, he also hath ceased from his
own works, as God did from his.
Let us labor therefore to enter into that rest.... (HEBREWS 4:9–11)

ക്ക&ക്ക&ക്ക&

Each day for the next week, reflect on what you *have* by considering a question or two along the following lines . . .

⋄ In the context of your present knowledge, what does the saying "life happens while we're busy doing something else" mean to you?

⋄ Describe a time when you started out to accomplish one goal and ended up with a wholly different (or somehow reshaped) set of objectives? When did you realize you were engaged with something novel and unexpected and what, if anything, did you learn from your detour or unplanned experience? If others were involved, what was the result of your change of direction on them?

⋄ To what degree do you sense that you like to keep tight control over life's happenings? In what way are *today's* events more — or less — peaceful for you, given your preferences?

We move beyond
false limits

Enlarge the place of thy tent . . .

Avocation leads us into a wilderness of trust and adventure. Holy work reflects Life's absorbing flame. If we
stay close to it, wide awake, it heats up and lights up all that
we do. Do you distrust unfamiliar feelings, like deep regret
or high excitement? Do you search for neatly packaged solutions or guarantees? Do you like your creative projects made
easy and predictable — replete with evenly spaced coffee-
breaks or planned out instructions thought through for you
by someone else for orderly understanding?

False assumptions about what it means to work with
passion account for years of aimless wandering. Let go of
confusion. Let the Holy Spirit teach you, bring all things
to remembrance and guide you to the outermost corners of
awareness — the Utter East, as C. S. Lewis called it.

Enlarge the place of thy tent,
and let them stretch forth the curtains of thine habitations:
spare not, lengthen thy cords, and strengthen thy stakes;
For thou shalt break forth on the right hand and on the left . . .

(ISAIAH 54:2–3)

๛ ๛ ๛ ๛ ๛ ๛

Each day for the next week, reflect on what you *have* by considering a question or two along the following lines . . .

๛ Describe a time when reading a line of Scripture or a delicately worded poem moved you toward the calm of "the outmost corners of awareness." What, if any, lasting benefits did that experience have on you?

๛ When has either commonplace experience or a spiritual epiphany taught you to move beyond what you imagined were your limits: fear, fatigue, the "I can't" sense, or what initially you thought was impossible interpersonal conflict? How have those sorts of lessons influenced your life?

๛ In terms of your life today, how do you interpret the phrase "Enlarge the place of your tent?" What do the words "tent" and "enlarge" signify to you. Over the short haul (e.g., today, this week) how might you honor (or affirm appropriately) that directive?

Our day is blessed

I will give thee places to walk . . .

Bit by intelligible bit, a vocation lets us express our healthiest instincts, our noblest desires. We commit to goals well beyond ourselves — beauty, tenacity, compassion. Or, perhaps we cut back. Doing less is often heroic, and that choice also blesses us. In small things and in large, we can attend to the haunting inner summons of our soul.

By injecting some lovely poetry-of-self into each day, we find our place amongst our fellows. We'll be discreetly kind to others through what we say or do or shed light on some supposedly dark problem. Tomorrow brightens as we do. *Today's* acts are blessed by honoring our high ideas of truth or affluence or service.

Thus saith the Lord of hosts;
If thou wilt walk in my ways, and if thou wilt keep my charge,
then thou shalt also judge my house, and shalt also keep my
  courts,
and I will give thee places to walk among these that stand by.

(ZECHARIAH 3:7)

᭰ᩥ ᭰ᩥ ᭰ᩥ ᭰ᩥ ᭰ᩥ ᭰ᩥ

Each day for the next week, reflect on what you *have* by considering a question or two along the following lines . . .

- ᭰ Specifically, as you anticipate the day directly in front of you — or as you review the prior day — what does "walking in the Lord's way" suggest to you?

- ᭰ Describe some nonintrusive and appropriate actions in which you might bless someone else's day, and — as you go through the coming week — consider how you might best acknowledge those who bless you.

- ᭰ What might it mean to you, your child, or your family to start a "Blessing Autobiography"? What do you suppose the effects might be if children or family members started keeping a log, photographs, quotations, and the like, of people, ideas, and growthful happenings that are a blessing to them?

We praise life

I will triumph in the works of thy hands . . .

E ach act of right livelihood engages us completely. A vocation calls for focus, well-managed attention — an encounter that kindles a healthful life. Our glad and whole-some involvements fire up mental strength, our heart's own competence, robust well-being.

To enjoy yourself today — as you haul groceries to your car or wait your turn in line — is to cheer up in "little" things so that all else improves. In the Lord there is no big or small, and our gladness *is* our praise.

It is a good thing to give thanks unto the Lord,
and to sing praises unto thy name, O most High:
To shew forth thy lovingkindness in the morning,
and thy faithfulness every night,
Upon an instrument of ten strings, and upon the psaltery;
upon the harp with a solemn sound.
For thou, Lord, hast made me glad through thy work:
I will triumph in the work of thy hands. (PSALM 92:1–4)

⊰⊱⊰⊱⊰⊱⊰⊱⊰⊱⊰⊱

Each day for the next week, reflect on what you *have* by considering a question or two along the following lines...

- ⊰ Thinking back on your pattern of praising others — or Life itself — what ten words or phrases best capture *your* manner of thanksgiving? Would your loved ones or closest working associates be surprised to hear you articulate your appreciation of, or compliment for, something they did?

- ⊰ Today, list three habits that you have or would like to cultivate that might praise some of the "inanimate" aspects of daily life: your home, garden, car, neighborhood, or nation. Who have you noticed acting in those ways and how appropriate or effective are their praiseful choices? At week's end, review your entire list to determine one or two habits of praise you might want to enhance.

We are joyfully engrossed

Thy God reigneth!

R aking dry, brown autumn leaves revives us when we're engrossed and self-vanishing in the task. Our vocation roots us jubilantly in each moment by offering us a meditation of sorts. When lax, lazy, or caught up in the quest for that perfect job, can we turn our attention back to what needs proper doing, right now?

Love aims us high. It dedicates us to being whatever's good or lasting beyond ourselves. It uplifts. We sense: "I *am* a teacher" (or an engineer or a parent). *Not,* "I wish I were one."

Joyful engagements unfold our best selves. As we faithfully translate our ephemeral visions into the practical present, beauty's substance arrives here and now, alive, at this moment. We *are* the lovely actuality we seek.

*How beautiful upon the mountains are the feet of him that
    bringeth good tidings, that publisheth peace;*
that bringeth good tidings of good, that publisheth salvation;
that saith unto Zion, Thy God reigneth! (ISAIAH 52:7)

Each day for the next week, reflect on what you *have* by
considering a question or two along the following lines...

- Name *one* thing you do each day that commands your
  full attention. Today, in what sense does your complete
  focus summon forth your best or most joyful self?

- During the upcoming day (and week, if possible), consider doing one more thing each day — washing the
  dishes? listening to your children, customers, or co-
  worker? paying your bills? — with full or, at minimum,
  improved attention, even if at first you don't feel like it.
  At the end of each day (or the week), evaluate the result
  of your efforts. What might you want to improve?

We draw forth what is good

Every tree is known by its own fruit...

Sincerity of service is a substantial power. It lets us reach out confidently for what seems rightfully ours: the well-timed execution of projects, the unique niche of belonging in the grand scheme of things. "Good feelings" come from drawing forth what's good within. That's our job: to consciously choose the good each day. We feel deserving when we watch ourselves behaving virtuously.

Some say that the moment they *felt* deserving was the moment that money, career, and friendships fell into place. Their own virtue — integrity, uprightness, and moral excellence — freed subjective worthiness and liberated their wit.

We know we can deliver the goods in everyday terms if, from the treasure of our depths, we call out and tangibly demonstrate what's good. The proof is in the pudding.

For a good tree bringeth not forth corrupt fruit;
neither doth a corrupt tree bring forth good fruit.
For every tree is known by his own fruit.
For of thorns men do not gather figs,
nor of a bramble bush gather they grapes.

(LUKE 6:43–44)

⊸⑥⊸⑥⊸⑥⊸⑥⊸⑥⊸⑥

Each day for the next week, reflect on what you *have* by considering a question or two along the following lines . . .

- How would you describe your "unique niche of belonging in the grand scheme of things"? How did that belonging come about? To what extent do you expect, celebrate, or mentally acknowledge the productive place you hold in life?

- Given your chores, meetings, or other obligations this day, what "good fruit" do you expect to bring forth? By week's end?

- To what extent does your customary or routine "good fruit" add to or enhance your place of belonging in the greater scheme of things? Should you want to enlarge the scope of your belonging, how might you multiply your gifts of "good fruit" in appropriate ways?

We are as a lamplight

Ye are the light of the world . . .

Holy workers don't huff and puff with prideful effort. Neither do they dramatize their struggles. Theirs is a self-assurance that others love receiving.

We *like* to be around the true-blue and the productive. We want to feel our associates' sincerity. Eagerly we hire those whose upbeat energy or inner radiance influences *us* for the better. In general, it's the reliable, constructive sorts who get our repeat business. And why not? Their shine is as a lamplight to *our* feet. Let us return the favor.

Ye are the light of the world.
A city that is set on a hill cannot be hid.
Neither do men light a candle and put it under a bushel, but on
*   a candlestick:*
and it giveth light unto all that are in the house.
Let your light so shine before men, that they may see your good
*   works, and glorify your Father which is in heaven.*

(MATTHEW 5:14–16)

👑👑👑👑

Each day for the next week, reflect on what you *have* by
considering a question or two along the following lines . . .

- Reflecting on your life to date, name a few individuals —
  family members, friends, colleagues, mentors or far-off,
  distant heroes — who have been "as a lamplight to your
  feet." What were they like and what did they do to have
  influenced you so positively?

- What traits do they have in common? What does that
  pattern of giving say to you about yourself, what you've
  needed, where you may be headed, and who you are?

- Reviewing the last twenty-four hours and/or the last
  week, to what extent do you think you've been a lamplight to others? What, when all is said and done, might
  be your best or most outstanding "lamplighting" attributes or actions? How do those traits or comport-
  ments influence your vocational choices?

We gain functional strength

Bring forth much fruit . . .

G ood judgment, discernment, cooperative life in community, freedom from dis-ease are all improved by
a vocation. We function well because we love to function.
Those beyond us profit from the risks we take or the disci-
plines we follow as we choose willingly to *be* "new wine." Not
we, but the Lord, makes the place of our feet glorious.

As we submit to Love's perfect authorship in us, small re-
linquishments produce great gains. We give up our limits, not
our dreams: We travel on planes when, previously, we feared
flight. Or we give speeches in public although, before, we
felt shy. Small deaths turn into larger Life and round us out
more perfectly. This means a vocation helps us find rightful
strength. We'll wake up early, watch our diet, exercise, or care
for a poodle. Embracing simple responsibilities — *functioning* easily and well and with intelligence — we'll consciously
choose this deed and the next and the next, as opportunities
to pour out stale useless acts in favor of that which would be
new wine — poured out through us.

Verily, verily, I say unto you, Except a corn of wheat fall into
  the ground and die, it abideth alone:
but if it die, it bringeth forth much fruit.
He that loveth his life shall lose it; and he that hateth his life in
  this world shall keep it unto life eternal.
If any man serve me, let him follow me; and where I am, there
  shall also my servant be:
if any man serve me, him will my Father honor. (JOHN 12:24–26)

୶ଈ ୶ଈ ୶ଈ ୶ଈ ୶ଈ ୶ଈ

Each day for the next week, reflect on what you *have* by
considering a question or two along the following lines ...

- ୶ In the last twenty-four hours, what small self-sacrifices
  or renunciations have resulted in your (or anyone else's)
  productive gain?

- ୶ During the day in front of you (and/or to the entire
  next week), what small sacrifices or renunciations might
  produce beneficial results?

- ୶ To what degree do you experience yourself as bringing
  forth "good fruit" in this fashion? How helpful might it
  be to begin a dialogue with your co-workers, your community of worship, or other community leaders about
  these issues — about, say, encouraging oneself and others
  to assess daily, weekly, or quarterly the "good fruit" they
  produce?

Finally, we have a sufficiency of good

You were set up from everlasting . . .

Some say a vocation reveals what it means to approach all things with a grateful heart. Others report feeling fulfilled. Finally they have a sense of sufficiency and use each task as if expressing a divine purpose, a true love.

One writer said, "My joy seems independent of conditions — buying a new car or keeping up with some friend. I *have* a life, my own life, and that blesses me." Ordinary events structure that satisfaction when life flows out of our anointed rebirth in Love.

Preparing a stew for our family or replacing a fence post are living gestures of our praise. These uncomplicated acts celebrate simple giving. We are a "firstfruit," sharing tirelessly our intellectual or technical prowess, or listening sympathetically while the neighbor's child bemoans her lost cat.

As we link up to others out of loving oneness with God, it goes well with us. And this is plenty.

The Lord possessed me in the beginning of his way,
before his works of old.
I was set up from everlasting, from the beginning . . .
When there were no depths, I was brought forth;
when there were no fountains abounding with water.
Before the mountains were settled, before the hills
was I brought forth. (PROVERBS 8:22–25)

❦❦❦❦❦❦

Each day for the next week, reflect on what you *have* by considering a question or two along the following lines . . .

❦ Describe a time when you've felt complete emotionally, felt that in God you were sufficient. What circumstances surrounded you at that time?

❦ To what extent is subjective completeness your experience today, this week, this year? That is, how often and when do you feel like all is right with your world and that, finally, you have a sufficiency of good?

❦ How might you celebrate your subjective sufficiency this day, this week, and gradually receive more of that blessing? Do you think the sense of having enough is a grace or that there's something more you must be, do, or have in order to experience that? To what extent might the sense of completeness further your ability to tackle "real-world problems"?

We grow radiantly ourselves

We have salt in ourselves . . .

Holy work is not necessarily linked to membership in some organized religion. We could be curmudgeons — not *always* brimming over with Goodie Two-Shoes cheer. We are, however, vibrantly spiritual: born again in the sheer stillness and purity of the Lord. When we're real, being a long-distance runner, a reporter, or a florist animates *our* essential nature, what we already are "from the beginning, when there were no depths." Being more real each day could make us tart, could well find us growing more biting, yet more flavorfully ourselves — warts and all.

When our choices reflect Love's purifying action in us, we are radiantly ourselves. Said one parent, "Being myself is no intellectual exercise. If my baby cries at midnight, I get up to see what's needed. Yes I grumble. *And* I get up. It's that simple."

Abiding in a consciousness of preexisting Love, we are called to be the self from which truth can emerge.

For every one shall be salted with fire,
and every sacrifice shall be salted with salt.
Salt is good: but if the salt have lost his saltness,
wherewith will ye season it?
Have salt in yourselves and have peace with one another.

(MARK 9:49–50)

෯෯෯෯෯෯෯

Each day for the next week, reflect on what you *have* by considering a question or two along the following lines . . .

෯ Today, how do you interpret — or conceive of — "Love's purifying action" in you? What has occurred over the course of your own life to purify, improve, or bless your attitudes and conduct, your character structure as a whole?

෯ Describe *your* "*salt*": that is, what aspects of character give flavor to your way of being, your relationships and achievements? Where does your "saltness" come from and to what degree does your vocation, your way of being and engagement with daily life, benefit from your saltness? Might a bit more — or less — salt improve your vocational life?

෯ Today, what does the following line mean to you: "*Every sacrifice shall be salted with salt?*"

We listen discerningly

The Lord is with you . . .

C onsciousness is *con*structive. With our productive
thoughts, words, and the simplest of choices, we structure our future. *Hearing* that we need to live with beauty
or mentor others frees us to choose those fulfillments, not
counterfeit substitutes.

Whatever we call prayer (and by whatever means we pray),
it brings oneness — oneness with the Kingdom within. We
listen discerningly to grasp the promise of Christ's unseen
substance, perhaps unformed yet mysteriously alive within.

A vocation lets us do nothing at times, be lighthearted,
even "lazy." In fact, indolent times are preparatory: These
ready us for tomorrow. In the stillness of fishing trips or
washing windows, we listen for directions for next steps.
The chance remark, the novel weekend seminar or required
college course becomes a significant tool of growth when received discerningly. In trust, we feel protected in both meek
acts and extravagant. In trust, our way of being gives witness
to Life's animating essence.

Ye shall not need to fight in this battle:
set yourselves, stand ye still, and see the salvation of the Lord
  with you . . .
fear not, nor be dismayed; tomorrow go out against them:
for the Lord will be with you. (2 CHRONICLES 20:17)

❧❧❧❧❧❧

Each day for the next week, reflect on what you *have* by considering a question or two along the following lines . . .

❧ Today, observe what it means to you to experience genuine — not counterfeit — success. Consider noting in your private journal the authentic fulfillment that you've had. List three times you "listened discerningly" to identify your satisfactions, past and present.

❧ How important is "standing still" to your day and your week's success? Exactly when and how — over the course of your normal experience — do you "stand still," listen discerningly, or feel that "the Lord is with you, guiding you, protecting you"?

We feel safe

Our life is founded on a rock . . .

A true vocation somehow settles us. We're being and doing God's will. Paradoxically, even during harsh storms — when, temporarily, we get rattled — the inner Treasure strengthens us. A single mother said, "When I'm fatigued and scattered, I think about my child, remember what she needs — what I *want* to do — and I'm blessed: In short order, I'm made strong — not through *my* power, but through the overarching sense of what needs doing, through me." That high intention orders us. Another person recast that blessing in a spiritual light when telling how he handled a grave surgery: "I was nervous but believe God works through doctors, too. Also, I knew that if my time was up, I'd be safe forever — in Heaven — and, totally accepting St. Paul's thought that 'to die is gain,' I rested easy, come what might."

Being simply ourselves (and being that as perfectly as possible) is enough, *is* our vocation — the holy work we are, a mission rich enough to produce a lifetime of reward. So does "a little one . . . become a thousand, and a small one a strong nation; I the Lord will hasten it" (Isa. 60:22).

A good man out of the good treasure of his heart
bringeth forth that which is good...
He is like a man which built an house, and digged deep,
and laid the foundation on a rock.... (LUKE 6:45–48)

Each day for the next week, reflect on what you *have* by considering a question or two along the following lines...

- Today, describe what you need or want to be, do, or have in order to "be the self you are, and be that perfectly," as St. Francis de Sales put it.

- To what extent are you able — or willing — to cultivate those attributes and actions? At day's end, describe your outcomes: What, today, did you bring forth from the treasure of your heart?

- What might be the consequences of your adopting a progressively authentic stance? That is, what do you suppose others — those you regard highly or rely on for belonging at home, at work, in community — will say or do if, progressively, you reveal the best self you are?

We are blessed to be a blessing

Yea, I have a goodly heritage . . .

A full encounter with whoever we really are and whatever we're doing is a form of gratitude. It is love. A baker noted, "My pumpkin pies are the best in town. Making them at Thanksgiving time is my prayer of sheer delight." We pay homage to Life by paying attention to our prayers of delight. That praiseful awareness celebrates our gift of life in God — our love or God.

As our work of baking pies or banjo playing blesses us, we become a blessing to others.

The Lord is the portion of mine inheritance and of my cup: thou maintainest my lot.
The lines are fallen unto me in pleasant places; yea, I have a goodly heritage. (PSALMS 16:5–6)

⋐⋐⋐⋐⋐⋐

Each day for the next week, reflect on what you *have* by considering a question or two along the following lines . . .

ᴥ Keep a list of the ways in which you have already been blessed to be a blessing. Consider not simply obvious gifts or material wealth, but also your subtle shades of uniqueness. If desirable, watch this day's television or movies and listen to the radio or to your friends with eye and ear turned toward the manner in which others are blessed to be a blessing. In sum, use your day and your week to build the muscles of your observational appreciation for the notion of "being blessed to be a blessing."

ᴥ Today, record at least three ways in which you actually do bless others by means of your blessings. Record how others bless you.

ᴥ Every evening before you retire, record at least seven ways in which — for that day — you've received your goodly heritage. (If you're unsure of what that phrase means, before starting the exercise reread the Parable of the Prodigal Son and then define the phrase "goodly heritage" for yourself.)

Summary: Why bother?
The blessings of a vocation

- We let go of old business and it kisses us goodbye,
- We make time for Beauty,
- Darkness departs,
- We accommodate eternity's plans,
- Now we stand in shining light,
- We gain our life,
- We sing a true song,
- We develop a perceptive faith,
- We use trials as stepping stones,
- We know how to rest,
- We move beyond false limits,
- Our day is blessed,
- We praise life,
- We are joyfully engrossed,
- We draw forth what is good,
- We are as a lamplight,
- We gain functional strength,
- Finally, we have a sufficiency of good,
- We grow radiantly ourselves,
- We listen discerningly,
- We feel safe,
- We are blessed to be a blessing.

Notes

1. Fr. Roch Kereszty, *If Today You Hear His Voice*, pamphlet.

2. Raimon Panikkar, "Nine Ways Not to Talk about God," *Cross Currents* (Summer 1997): 149–53.

3. Oswald Chambers, *My Utmost for His Highest* (Uhrichsville, Ohio: Barbour and Co., 1953), 16–18

4. James Thurber, "The Mouse and the Money," as cited in *The International Thesaurus of Quotations*, comp. Rhoda Thomas Tripp (New York: Thomas Crowell, 1970), 19.

5. Jill Haak Adels, *The Wisdom of the Saints* (New York: Oxford University Press, 1987), 73.

6. Robert Frost, "Two Tramps in Mid-Time," as cited in *Bartlett's Quotations*.

7. Marsha Sinetar, *A Way without Words* (Mahwah, N.J.: Paulist Press, 1992).

8. Ibid., 16.

9. John Wesley, *The Forbes Scrapbook of Thoughts on the Business Life* (New York: Forbes, Inc., 1968), 500.

10. G. K. Chesterton, *Saint Thomas Aquinas* (New York: Image Books, 1956), chapter 1, "The Dumb Ox."

11. Persian proverb, as cited in *International Thesaurus of Quotations*, 289.7.

12. Brother Lawrence, *The Practice of the Presence of God* (Old Tappan, N.J.: Spire Books, Fleming Revell Co., 1958, 1980).

13. Albert Camus, as cited in *International Thesaurus of Quotations*, 868.5.

14. Brother Lawrence, *The Practice of the Presence of God*, 25.

15. Peter Browning, *John Muir, in His Own Words: A Book of Quotations* (Lafayette, Calif.: Great West Books, 1988), 25.

16. Mark Twain, as cited in *International Thesaurus of Quotations*, 717.33.

17. Brother Lawrence, *The Practice of the Presence of God*, 20.

18. Gilbert Shaw, *The Christian Solitary* (Fairacres, Oxford: SLG Press, 1969), 1.

Scripture Index

And the Spirit and the bride say, Come.
And let him that heareth say, Come.
And let him that is athirst come.
And whosoever will, let him take the water of life freely.

(REVELATION 22:17)